Cooking for Myself

Gage Publishing
Published in agreement with Les Editions internationales Alain Stanké,
Montréal, Québec.

Original title: *Je Cuisine Pour Moi*
Cover photo: Photolex

Les Editions internationales Alain Stanké
Copyright © Ottawa, 1976

Gage Publishing
Copyright © 1978

Canadian Cataloguing in Publication Data
Beaulieu, Mirelle, 1934-
Cooking for Myself
Translation of Je cuisine pour moi.
Includes index.

ISBN 0-7715-9435-6 pa.
1. Cookery. I. Title.
TX652.B34813   641.5'61   C78-001230-5

Printed and bound in Canada.

 2 3 4 J D 81 80

COOKING
FOR MYSELF

(Je Cuisine Pour Moi)

MIRELLE BEAULIEU

Macmillan of Canada
A Division of Gage Publishing Limited
Toronto, Canada

Contents

Foreword

Cooking for a family or for friends can be an enjoyable experience. You can let yourself go and be creative. And the crowning compliment of satisfied faces and sighs of appreciation around the table rewards your efforts.

When you're cooking for yourself, however, without the stimulation of shared pleasure, enthusiasm and imagination fly out the window. "It's not worth the bother," you tell yourself. "Besides, who needs a mess of pots and pans!" So you open a can or throw together some unappetizing concoction and let it go at that. Dull, dull, dull—and, usually, unnutritious.

But cooking a tasty meal for yourself doesn't have to involve time-consuming and complicated preparation. You don't have to end up with a sinkful of messy dishes. The recipes in this cookbook are easy to follow, quick to prepare, and also, most important, tasty and nutritious with a minimum of muss and fuss.

Bon appétit!

Appetizers

Apple with ham stuffing

1 medium apple

1 tsp. lemon juice

1 slice cooked ham, diced

1 tbsp. chopped nuts

1 tbsp. finely chopped celery

2 tbsp. whipping cream

Salt and pepper

Pinch of chopped chervil

Core the apple and scoop out as much pulp as you can, being careful not to break the skin.
Cut up the pulp in small pieces and sprinkle with lemon juice.
Mix the diced ham, chopped apple, nuts, and celery.
Stir in the whipping cream.
Add salt and pepper to taste.
Fill the apple shell with the mixture and sprinkle chopped chervil on top.
Serve well chilled.

Asparagus and cucumber with chervil

3 asparagus tips, cooked

8 thin slices of cucumber, unpeeled

2 tbsp. sour cream

1 tsp. lemon juice

Salt and pepper to taste

1/4 tsp. chopped chervil

Place the asparagus tips in the centre of a small plate and arrange the cucumber slices around.

Mix the sour cream, lemon juice, salt, and pepper and pour over.

Sprinkle with chopped chervil.

Asparagus and ham roll

3 tbsp. whipping cream

1 tsp. prepared mustard

½ tsp. lemon juice

1 hard-cooked egg, finely chopped

½ tsp. minced chives

¼ tsp. minced parsley

¼ tsp. minced chervil

Salt and pepper

1 slice cooked ham

3 asparagus tips, cooked

Lettuce leaf

Mix the first nine ingredients.

Roll the asparagus tips in the slice of cooked ham.

Place on a lettuce leaf on a small plate and pour the dressing over.

Serve well chilled.

Asparagus hors-d'oeuvre

½ cup cooked asparagus, cut in pieces ½ inch long

2 tbsp. mayonnaise

1 tsp. ketchup

Pinch of cayenne pepper

1 small tomato, sliced

6 cucumber slices, peeled

2 tbsp. salad oil

1 tbsp. lemon juice

Salt and pepper to taste

Lettuce leaves

1 hard-cooked egg, cut into quarters

3 asparagus spears, cooked

1 tsp. chopped chives

Mix the cut up asparagus with the mayonnaise, ketchup, and cayenne pepper. Chill.

Marinate the slices of tomato and cucumber in a dressing made of the oil, lemon juice, salt, and pepper. Chill.

Arrange a bed of lettuce leaves on a plate. Place the asparagus mixture in the centre and surround it with the tomato and cucumber slices and the egg wedges.

Garnish with asparagus spears and sprinkle with finely chopped chives.

You can use the leftover asparagus in the following recipes:
Asparagus and cucumber with chervil, page 14
Fillet of sole with asparagus, page 117
Asparagus with tomato sauce, page 139
Asparagus au gratin, page 138

Cold vegetable plate

¼ cup grated carrot

¼ cup chopped celery

¼ cup diced beets

1 hard-cooked egg, chopped

2 tbsp. whipping cream

½ tsp. prepared mustard

1 tsp. lemon juice

Salt and pepper

Arrange the vegetables in sections on a small plate.

Sprinkle the chopped egg over.

Blend the cream, mustard, and lemon juice and pour the mixture over the vegetables and egg.

Salt and pepper to taste.

Serve well chilled.

Cucumber with chives

½ cup cucumber, peeled and thinly sliced

Salt and pepper

1 tsp. lemon juice

1 tbsp. sour cream

1 tsp. chopped chives

Lightly salt the cucumber slices and let stand to draw out the liquid.

Drain well, pressing out excess moisture.

Mix in the lemon juice and sour cream.

Season generously with freshly ground black pepper.

Sprinkle with chopped chives.

Serve cold.

Cucumber hors-d'oeuvre

1 tbsp. salad oil

1 tsp. vinegar

¼ tsp. minced chives

Salt and pepper to taste

5 cucumber slices, peeled

¼ cup radishes, sliced

2 canned asparagus tips, drained

⅓ cup finely chopped lettuce

Make a vinaigrette dressing by mixing the oil, vinegar, chives, salt, and pepper in a jar with a tight-fitting lid and shaking well.
Arrange the vegetables in sections on a small plate.
Pour the vinaigrette over.
Serve cold.

Cucumber with tomato dressing

¼ cup tomato, peeled and chopped

1 clove garlic, crushed

2 tbsp. salad oil

1 tsp. vinegar

Pinch of basil

Salt and pepper

6 thin slices of cucumber, peeled

1 shallot, finely chopped

Chopped parsley

Mash the chopped tomato with a fork and mix with the crushed garlic, oil, vinegar and basil to make a thick sauce.

Add salt and pepper to taste.

Place the cucumber slices on a small plate. Pour the tomato sauce over.

Sprinkle with finely chopped shallot and parsley.

Refrigerate for about one hour before serving.

Grapefruit and crab cocktail

½ grapefruit

½ cup crabmeat

1 tbsp. mayonnaise

1 tsp. lemon juice

Pinch of cayenne pepper

1 tsp. minced parsley

Carefully scoop out the flesh from the grapefruit half. Rinse the shell in cold water and turn upside down to drain.

Cut the flesh of the grapefruit into small pieces and mix with the crabmeat.

Add the mayonnaise, lemon, and cayenne pepper and mix well.

Fill the grapefruit shell with the mixture and sprinkle with finely chopped parsley.

Serve well chilled.

Ham and cabbage salad

⅓ cup grated cabbage

1 tbsp. diced apple

2 tsp. chopped nuts

2 tbsp. cooked ham, diced

1 tbsp. sweet pickles, chopped

1 tsp. minced chives

1 tsp. vinegar

1 tbsp. salad oil

Salt and pepper to taste

Mix the first six ingredients.
Blend the vinegar, oil, salt, and pepper and pour the dressing over the salad, mixing it in well.
Serve well chilled.

Ham and rice salad

1 tbsp. ketchup
Pinch of cayenne pepper
Salt and pepper to taste
1 tbsp. mayonnaise
⅓ cup cooked rice
1 slice cooked ham, cut into strips
2 tbsp. canned mushrooms, drained and sliced
2 tbsp. unpeeled cucumber, diced
1 tsp. minced chives
2 tsp. lemon juice
2 – 3 lettuce leaves
1 hard-cooked egg, cut into quarters

Blend the ketchup, cayenne pepper, salt, pepper, and mayonnaise.
Mix the rice, ham strips, mushrooms, cucumber, chives, and lemon juice.
Place the mixture on a bed of lettuce leaves, garnish with egg wedges, and
pour the dressing over.
Serve cold.

To use the rest of the canned mushrooms, see the following recipes:
Beef with mushroom sauce, page 51
Hamburger steak with mushroom sauce, page 56
Veal scallop with cream sauce, page 93
Chicken with mushrooms, page 103
Rice with mushrooms, page 228

Ham salad

1 slice cooked ham

½ cup chopped celery

1 tbsp. chopped nuts

1 tbsp. mayonnaise

1 tsp. prepared mustard

Salt and pepper to taste

Chopped chervil

Cut the slice of cooked ham into thin strips.
Put the ham strips, chopped celery, and nuts into a small salad bowl.
Blend the mayonnaise, mustard, salt, and pepper and pour the dressing over the salad, mixing it in well.
Sprinkle lightly with chopped chervil.
Serve very cold.

Lettuce with hard-cooked egg

1 hard-cooked egg

1 tsp. prepared mustard

Salt and pepper to taste

2 tbsp. salad oil

2 tsp. vinegar

1 cup shredded lettuce

Mash the hard-cooked egg yolk and mix it with the mustard, salt, pepper, oil, and vinegar to make a smooth dressing.

Place the shredded lettuce in a small salad bowl.

Add the dressing and toss lightly.

Garnish with slivers of hard-cooked egg white.

Serve very cold.

Mortadella sausage and radishes

1 tsp. prepared mustard

3 tsp. salad oil

1 tsp. wine vinegar

Salt and pepper to taste

1/4 tsp. minced parsley

1/4 tsp. chopped chives

1/2 cup diced mortadella sausage

1/2 cup sliced radishes

Mix the mustard, oil, vinegar, salt, and pepper. Add the chopped parsley and chives.

Pour the dressing over the radishes and mortadella sausage. Toss lightly and refrigerate until ready to serve.

Rice and green peas

1/3 cup cooked rice

1/4 cup canned green peas, drained

1 tbsp. sweet pickles, finely chopped

2 tsp. prepared mustard

1 tsp. salad oil

1 tsp. vinegar

Combine the rice, peas, and pickles and set aside.
Blend the mustard, oil, and vinegar and gently mix into the first mixture.
Serve very cold.

To use the rest of the canned peas, see the following recipes:
Minted peas, page 150
Green peas and onions, page 147

Rice with shrimp

⅓ cup water

⅓ cup quick-cooking rice

⅓ cup small shrimp, cooked

2 stuffed olives, cut in half

1 tsp. vinegar

1 tbsp. salad oil

½ tsp. prepared mustard

Salt and pepper to taste

1 small tomato, cut in quarters

Cook the rice according to directions on the package.

Mix the shrimp, olives, and cooked rice.

Blend the vinegar, oil, mustard, salt, and pepper and add it to the shrimp mixture, tossing lightly.

Garnish with tomato wedges.

Shrimp cocktail

½ cup cooked shrimp

1 tbsp. cognac

1 tbsp. mayonnaise

½ tsp. prepared mustard

1 tsp. ketchup

Pinch of cayenne pepper

Lettuce leaf

Place the shrimp in a small dish and sprinkle with cognac.

Combine the mayonnaise, mustard, ketchup, and cayenne pepper.

Pour the sauce over the shrimp and mix well.

Serve on a lettuce leaf.

Tomato with egg slices

1 large tomato

1 hard-cooked egg, sliced

1 tbsp. salad oil

1 tsp. vinegar

½ tsp. prepared mustard

Salt and pepper to taste

½ tsp. minced chives

Cut the tomato in thick vertical slices, being careful not to cut all the way through.

Salt the sliced tomato and let the excess juice drain out.

Place slices of hard-cooked egg between the tomato slices.

Mix the oil, vinegar, mustard, salt, and pepper and blend thoroughly.

Pour the dressing over the tomato and egg combination.

Sprinkle with minced chives.

Tomato and sour cream

| 1 large tomato, cut in half |
| 1 lettuce leaf |
| 1 tbsp. sour cream |
| 1 tbsp. chopped shallot |
| Salt and pepper |
| Minced parsley |

Place the tomato halves on a lettuce leaf.

Combine the sour cream and chopped shallot and place a spoonful on top of each tomato half.

Sprinkle lightly with salt and generously with pepper.

Garnish with minced parsley.

Refrigerate at least an hour before serving.

Tomato stuffed with cucumber

1 medium tomato

1 tsp. prepared mustard

1 tsp. vinegar

1 tbsp. salad oil

¼ tsp. tarragon

Salt and pepper

½ cup peeled cucumber, diced

1 lettuce leaf

1 hard-cooked egg

Slice the top off the tomato, scoop out the inside, sprinkle lightly with salt, and invert to drain. Let stand about ten minutes.

Blend the mustard with the vinegar and oil to make a smooth sauce. Add the tarragon, salt, and pepper and mix in the diced cucumber.

Stuff the tomato with the cucumber mixture and place on a lettuce leaf.

Top with a slice of egg and a pinch of tarragon.

Chop the rest of the egg and sprinkle over as a garnish.

Tomato vinaigrette

1 tomato

1 lettuce leaf

Salt and pepper

1 shallot, finely chopped

¼ tsp. minced parsley

1 tbsp. oil

1 tsp. vinegar

1 garlic clove, crushed

1 tsp. sugar

¼ tsp. celery seed

¼ tsp. prepared mustard

Cut the tomato in thick slices and arrange on a leaf of lettuce.
Season with salt and pepper.
Sprinkle with chopped shallot and parsley.
Combine with remaining ingredients, blend thoroughly, and pour the vinaigrette over the tomato slices.
Serve cold.

Tuna fish and carrot salad

⅓ cup tuna fish

1 small carrot, grated

1 tbsp. minced shallot

1 tsp. prepared mustard

1 tsp. lemon juice

2 tbsp. salad oil

Salt and pepper to taste

1 tsp. chopped parsley

Mix the tuna fish, grated carrot, and minced shallot.
Blend the mustard, lemon juice, oil, salt, and pepper and pour the dressing
over, mixing it in well.
Sprinkle with chopped parsley.
Serve cold.

You can use the rest of the canned tuna in the recipe for:
Tuna fish omelette, page 133

Vegetable hors-d'oeuvre

¼ cup shredded lettuce

¼ cup diced beets

¼ cup grated carrot

2 tbsp. whipping cream

1 tsp. prepared mustard

1 tbsp. lemon juice

Salt and pepper to taste

1 tsp. chopped chervil

2 stuffed olives

Arrange the vegetables in sections on a plate.

Blend the whipping cream, mustard, lemon juice, and salt and pepper.

Pour the dressing over the vegetables, sprinkle chopped chervil over, and garnish with stuffed olives.

Soups

Cheesy cream of chicken

2 tbsp. grated carrot

1 tbsp. minced onion

1 tbsp. butter or margarine

$\frac{1}{2}$ cup canned cream of chicken soup, undiluted

$\frac{1}{2}$ cup water

$\frac{1}{2}$ tsp. Worcestershire sauce

Salt and pepper

2 tbsp. grated Cheddar cheese

Sauté the carrot and onion in butter until tender but not brown.

Add the cream of chicken soup, water, and Worcestershire sauce and bring to a rapid boil, stirring.

Remove from heat and season with salt and pepper.

Add the grated cheese and stir until melted.

Use the rest of the canned cream of chicken soup in the recipe for:

Chicken supreme, page 106

Consommé with lemon

1 tsp. instant chicken bouillon base

1 cup boiling water

2 slices lemon

Pinch of saffron

Pinch of mixed herbs

Put the first four ingredients in a saucepan and bring to a rolling boil. Boil for one minute.

When ready to serve, sprinkle with mixed herbs.

Cream of carrot

⅓ cup finely diced carrots

½ cup chicken bouillon

2 tsp. butter

2 tsp. flour

⅓ cup light cream

Salt and pepper

1 tsp. minced parsley

Cook the diced carrots in the chicken bouillon for 5 – 6 minutes, or until tender. Drain, reserving the cooking liquid, and mash. Set aside.

Melt the butter. When it stops foaming, stir in the flour.

Gradually add the cooking liquid, stirring.

Stir in the mashed carrots and bring to a gentle boil.

Slowly add the cream and simmer over low heat, being careful not to let it boil, until piping hot.

Season with salt and pepper and sprinkle with minced parsley.

Cream of Cheddar

¼ cup finely chopped onion

1 tbsp. butter or margarine

1 tsp. flour

¾ cup milk

Salt and pepper

¼ cup grated Cheddar cheese

Chopped parsley

Sauté the onion in butter until soft but not brown.

Stir in the flour, then add the milk, all at once.

Season with salt and pepper.

Bring to a boil, stirring.

Remove from the heat, add the cheese, and stir until the cheese is completely melted.

Sprinkle with chopped parsley.

Cream of lettuce

½ cup chicken bouillon

½ cup finely chopped lettuce

¼ cup sliced onion

2 tsp. butter

2 tsp. flour

½ cup milk

Salt and pepper

Chopped parsley

Bring the chicken bouillon to a rolling boil.

Add the lettuce and onion, lower the heat, cover, and let simmer for 15 minutes.

Purée in an electric blender or press through a sieve. Set aside.

Melt the butter and stir in the flour.

Add the milk and cook, stirring, until smooth and thickened.

Add the lettuce purée, season with salt and pepper, and heat for 2 – 3 minutes.

Sprinkle lightly with minced parsley and serve.

Cream of tomato

1 tbsp. diced bacon

1 tbsp. butter or margarine

2 tbsp. finely chopped celery

1 tbsp. minced onion

1 tsp. flour

¼ cup canned tomatoes, mashed

½ cup water

2 tbsp. white wine

1 tsp. instant chicken bouillon base

Cook the diced bacon until crisp. Set aside.
Sauté the celery and onion in the butter until tender but not brown.
Sprinkle flour over and stir in.
Add the tomatoes, water, wine, and bouillon base and cook over moderate heat, stirring, until the mixture begins to thicken.
Reduce heat and continue cooking 5 minutes longer, stirring occasionally.
Serve with crisp bacon bits sprinkled over.

Instant cream of Cheddar

½ cup canned Cheddar soup

½ cup table cream

2 tbsp. sherry

Put the ingredients in a small saucepan and cook over low heat, stirring, until the soup is hot.

The rest of the canned Cheddar soup can be used as a sauce for vegetables.

Shrimp bisque

1 tbsp. flour

1 cup milk

1 tbsp. butter or margarine

2 – 3 drops Tabasco sauce

Salt to taste

½ cup small shrimp, cooked

1 tbsp. sherry

Put the flour into the top half of a double boiler and gradually stir in the milk.
Add the butter, Tabasco sauce, and salt.
Cook over low heat, stirring, until the sauce thickens.
Add the shrimp and sherry and continue cooking for a few minutes, until
heated through.

Tarragon tomato

2 tsp. butter or margarine

1 tbsp. minced onion

1 tbsp. finely chopped celery

¾ cup tomato juice

2 – 3 drops Tabasco sauce

¼ tsp. sugar

1 tsp. tarragon

Salt and pepper to taste

Cook the onion and celery in melted butter until tender but not brown.
Add the rest of the ingredients, stir, and bring to a boil.
Let simmer for a few minutes.

Meats

Beef with mushroom sauce

2 tbsp. flour

6 – 8 oz. beef, cut in 1-inch cubes

1 tbsp. butter or margarine

¼ cup finely chopped onion

1 crushed garlic clove

⅓ cup canned consommé, undiluted

¼ cup sliced mushrooms

¼ tsp. basil

Salt and pepper to taste

2 tbsp. dry white wine

Dredge the beef cubes in flour.
Heat the butter in a frying pan and brown the meat.
Add the onions and garlic and cook 1 – 2 minutes, stirring.
Add the consommé, mushrooms, basil, salt, and pepper.
Cook, covered, over low heat for about an hour, or until the meat is tender.
Stir occasionally to prevent sticking.
When the meat is almost cooked, add the wine.
Serve with rice and parsley butter (see page 66).

To use the rest of the canned consommé, see:
Pan-broiled steak, page 59
Or, add 1 – 2 tablespoons of sherry and a pinch of rosemary or basil, heat, and serve piping hot.

Cheeseburger

6 oz. ground beef

1 tbsp. minced onion

Pinch of paprika

1 tsp. chopped parsley

1 tsp. Worchestershire sauce

Salt and pepper to taste

1 tbsp. butter

1 cheese slice

2 slices side bacon

½ hamburger bun, toasted

3 tbsp. chili sauce, heated

Mix the beef, onion, paprika, parsley, Worcestershire sauce, salt, and pepper and shape into meat patties.

Place the cheese slice between the patties.

Wrap the bacon slices around the double patty and tie with string.

Fry in hot butter for 5 – 10 minutes, or to the degree of doneness you prefer.

Place on toasted hamburger bun and pour heated chili sauce over.

Hamburger, French style

¼ lb. ground beef

1 tbsp. butter or margarine

1 minced garlic clove

1 slice French bread, ½-inch thick

2 – 3 slices of tomato

Shape the meat into a patty the same size as the slice of bread.

Melt the butter in a pan, add the garlic, and cook for 1 – 2 minutes.

Add the meat patty and cook for 2 – 3 minutes on each side.

Season with salt and pepper.

Pour the garlic butter over the toasted bread, place the hamburger on top, and garnish with tomato slices.

Hamburger with sour cream sauce

$1/4$ lb. ground round steak

1 tbsp. butter or margarine

1 tbsp. chopped onion

2 tbsp. ketchup

1 tsp. vinegar

$1/4$ tsp. dry mustard

Salt and pepper to taste

2 tbsp. sour cream

$1/2$ hamburger bun, toasted

Brown the ground round steak with the onion in hot butter. Stir in the ketchup, vinegar, mustard, salt, and pepper.

Cover and cook over low heat for 4 – 5 minutes.

Stir in the sour cream and heat just to the boiling point. Do not let the sauce boil, or it will curdle.

Serve on toasted hamburger bun.

Hamburger steak Lorraine

¼ cup chopped onion

1 tbsp. oil

¼ lb. ground round steak

2 tbsp. tomato paste

1 tbsp. breadcrumbs

Salt and pepper to taste

2 slices side bacon

1 tbsp. butter or margarine

Mushroom sauce

Sauté the onion in the oil.

Mix the ground steak, tomato paste, breadcrumbs, salt, and pepper and shape into two patties.

Spread the sautéed onion on one patty and put the second patty on top. Wrap the slices of bacon around the double-decker hamburger and tie with string.

Melt the butter in the same pan and cook the patty 3 – 4 minutes on each side, or until cooked to your degree of doneness.

To serve, untie the string and spoon mushroom sauce over.

See page 220 for the recipe for mushroom sauce.

Hamburger steak with mushroom sauce

6 oz. ground round steak

2 tbsp. chopped onion

Salt and pepper to taste

1 tbsp. butter or margarine

⅓ cup canned mushrooms, drained and sliced

1 tbsp. flour

1 tsp. instant beef bouillon base

½ cup liquid from canned mushrooms

Mix the ground steak, onion, salt, and pepper and shape into a hamburger patty.

Cook on both sides in hot butter over moderate heat for about 10 minutes.

Remove from the pan and keep hot.

Sauté the mushrooms in the same pan. Stir in the flour.

Add the beef bouillon base dissolved in the mushroom liquid and bring to a rapid boil, stirring. Cook until the sauce is thickened.

Place the hamburger steak on a heated plate, spoon the sauce over, and serve.

Hawaiian hamburger

¼ lb. ground beef

Salt and pepper

1 pineapple slice

1 tbsp. brown sugar

1 tbsp. ketchup

1 tsp. prepared mustard

1 hamburger bun, toasted

Preheat oven to 500°F.

Season the beef with salt and pepper and shape into two hamburger patties.

Place the pineapple slice between the patties and bake for 5 minutes.

Remove from oven, turn over, and cover with sauce made by mixing brown sugar, ketchup, and mustard.

Return to oven and bake 5 minutes longer.

Serve on toasted hamburger bun.

To use the rest of the canned pineapple slices, see the following recipes:

Broiled ham with pineapple, page 71
Pineapple desserts, pages 207-210

Minute steak

1 tbsp. oil

1 minute steak

Garlic salt and pepper

2 tbsp. butter or margarine

1 tsp. lemon juice

¼ tsp. dry mustard

1 tsp. Worcestershire sauce

2 tsp. chopped shallot

Heat the oil in a frying pan or skillet.

Cook the steak for 2 – 3 minutes on each side.

Season with garlic salt and pepper to taste.

Remove from pan and keep hot.

Drain the fat from the pan, melt the butter, and add the remaining ingredients.

Heat, stirring. Pour over the steak.

Pan-broiled steak

⅓ cup sliced mushrooms	
¼ cup green pepper, cut in strips	
1 small onion, sliced	
1 tbsp. oil	
2 tbsp. butter or margarine	
1 portion round steak	
2 tbsp. canned consommé, undiluted	
2 tbsp. red wine	

Cook the mushrooms, green pepper, and onion in the oil and 1 tablespoon butter until tender.
Push them to one side of the pan or skillet and add the remaining tablespoon of butter.
Cook the steak in the heated butter to the desired degree of doneness.
Transfer to a heated plate, garnish with the vegetable mixture, and keep hot.
Deglaze the pan with the consommé and wine, stirring vigorously with a wooden spoon to scrape up all the browned juices stuck to the pan. Pour this sauce over the steak.

Suggestion for using the rest of the canned consommé:
Mushroom sauce, page 220

Steak Diane

1 sirloin steak, $\frac{1}{3}$-inch thick

$\frac{1}{4}$ tsp. dry mustard

Salt and pepper to taste

1 shallot, chopped

2 tbsp. butter or margarine

2 tbsp. lemon juice

1 tsp. Worcestershire sauce

1 tsp. minced chives

Season the steak with a mixture of the mustard, salt, and pepper.

Brown the steak with the chopped shallot in hot butter, 1 – 2 minutes on each side, or to the desired degree of doneness.

Remove the steak from the skillet and keep hot.

Deglaze the pan with the lemon juice and Worcestershire sauce, scraping the bottom of the pan with a wooden spoon to get up all the flavorful brown bits.

Add the chives and pour the sauce over the steak.

Steak with mushroom sauce

1 portion round steak

2 tbsp. butter or margarine

Salt and pepper

¼ cup water

1 small onion, sliced

½ cup cream of mushroom soup, undiluted

1 tsp. chopped parsley

Brown the steak in hot butter for about 10 minutes.

Season with salt and pepper.

Add the water and onion, cover, and cook for 25 – 30 minutes, or until the meat is tender. Add more water as required.

Remove meat from pan and keep hot.

Heat the mushroom soup in the same pan over low heat, stirring.

Pour the sauce over the steak and sprinkle with chopped parsley.

To make cream of mushroom soup, add a little milk and chopped parsley to the remainder of the contents of the can, heat, and serve.

Steak with shallot sauce

1 tbsp. butter or margarine

1 tbsp. HP sauce

1 shallot, finely chopped

¼ tsp. Worcestershire sauce

Salt and pepper to taste

1 minute steak

1 slice French bread, 1-inch thick

Blend the butter, HP sauce, shallot, Worcestershire sauce, salt, and pepper and cook over low heat.

Cook the steak in a hot skillet, one minute on each side.

Dip the toasted bread into the sauce, put on a heated plate, place the steak on top, and pour the sauce over.

Stuffed green pepper

1 large green pepper

¼ lb. ground beef

¼ cup cooked rice

2 tbsp. chopped onion

1 tsp. Worcestershire sauce

Salt and pepper

¼ cup tomato sauce

Preheat oven to 350°F.

Cut the top off the stem end of the green pepper and a thin slice off the other end so that it will stay upright.

Remove the seeds and membrane, being careful not to break the shell.

Cook the pepper in salted, boiling water for 5 minutes. Drain well.

Mix the ground beef, rice, onion, Worcestershire sauce, and 2 tablespoons of the tomato sauce. Season with salt and pepper.

Stuff the pepper with the mixture and place in a small casserole or baking dish.

Pour the remaining tomato sauce over, cover, and bake for 30 – 35 minutes, basting occasionally.

To use the rest of the canned tomato sauce, see the following recipes:

Sausage and macaroni casserole, page 84

Baked rigatoni, page 159

Baked lamb chops

1 egg

1 tbsp. milk

Salt and pepper to taste

1/4 tsp. Worcestershire sauce

1/4 cup crushed cornflakes

2 lamb chops

Preheat oven to 375°F.

Beat the egg with the milk, salt, pepper, and Worcestershire sauce.

Dip the chops in the mixture, then coat with cornflake crumbs.

Place the chops in a well-buttered casserole dish and bake for 25 – 30 minutes, or until done.

Broiled lamb chops provençal

3 tsp. breadcrumbs

1 tsp. chopped parsley

2 garlic cloves, crushed

Salt and pepper to taste

1 medium tomato, halved

1 tbsp. butter or margarine

2 lamb chops

Preheat oven to 500°F.

Mix the breadcrumbs, parsley, garlic, salt, and pepper.

Sprinkle the seasoned breadcrumbs over the tomato halves, dot with butter, and bake for 15 – 20 minutes.

Broil the lamb chops on a hot, lightly oiled broiling pan, 4 – 5 minutes on each side.

The chops can also be pan-broiled in a hot skillet, in a little oil and butter.

Grilled lamb chops and green peas

2 lamb chops

Salt and pepper to taste

1 tbsp. butter or margarine

1 small onion, cut in rings

½ cup canned green peas, drained

1 tsp. mint jelly

Salt and pepper the lamb chops and grill in a hot, oiled skillet or preheated broiler.

While the chops are cooking, sauté the onion rings in the butter.

Add the green peas and mint jelly and cook over low heat for 3 – 4 minutes.

Serve the chops garnished with a dollop of parsley butter and arrange the vegetables around.

Parsley butter:

2 tsp. butter or margarine

1 tsp. chopped parsley

Mix until well blended.

To use the rest of the canned peas, see the following recipes:
Rice and green peas, page 27
Green peas and onions, 147

Lamb chops with rice

2 lamb chops

Salt and pepper

1 tbsp. butter or margarine

¼ cup long-grain rice

¼ cup orange juice

½ cup chicken soup with rice

1 tbsp. brown sugar

½ tsp. prepared mustard

¼ tsp. Worcestershire sauce

Preheat oven to 350°F.

Season the chops with salt and pepper and brown in hot butter.

Mix the rice, orange juice, and soup and pour into a casserole dish.

Place the browned chops on top and bake 20 – 25 minutes.

Blend the brown sugar, mustard, and Worcestershire sauce and brush the chops with the mixture.

Continue cooking 10 – 15 minutes longer, or until the chops are tender.

Lamb shish kebabs

5 or 6 cubes of lamb

¼ cup French dressing

2 small whole onions, canned

4 pineapple cubes, canned

3 green pepper squares

Marinate the cubes of meat in the French dressing in a covered container for about two hours.

Remove the meat from the marinade and place on a skewer, alternating the lamb cubes with the onions, pineapple, and green pepper.

Brush with the marinade and cook under a hot, oiled broiler for 5 – 7 minutes. Brush the other side with the marinade and broil another 5 minutes, or until the meat is tender.

Serve with rice and parsley butter (see page 66).

The rest of the canned pineapple can be used for:
Chicken Catalina, page 101

Lamb shish kebabs with mixed herbs

6 cubes of lamb shoulder

4 cubes of side bacon

2 cherry tomatoes

¼ cup oil

1 tbsp. vinegar

Salt and pepper to taste

Pinch of thyme

Pinch of rosemary

Arrange the first three ingredients on a skewer, beginning and ending with a cherry tomato and alternating the cubes of lamb and bacon.

Mix the oil, vinegar, salt, pepper, thyme, and rosemary and marinate the kebab in the mixture for at least ¾ hour.

Preheat broiler until very hot and broil the kebab for 4 – 5 minutes on each side.

Serve with rice and parsley butter (see page 66).

Baked ham roll

1 small leek

1 tbsp. butter

1 tbsp. flour

½ cup milk

Salt and pepper

Pinch of nutmeg

¼ cup grated Gruyère cheese

2 slices of cooked ham

Preheat oven to 500°F.

Wash the white part of the leek, drain, and tie with string or thread. Cook in boiling, salted water for 10 minutes.

Melt the butter in a small saucepan, add the flour, and cook, stirring, for about a minute.

Blend in the milk and ¼ cup of leek stock. Season with salt, pepper, and nutmeg and cook, stirring, until the sauce begins to thicken.

Remove from heat, add half the cheese, and stir until melted.

When the leek is cooked, drain, remove the thread, and roll it up in one of the ham slices. Cut the other slice of ham into small pieces and place them in the bottom of a small, buttered gratin or baking dish. Place the ham roll-up on top and pour the sauce over. Sprinkle with the rest of the grated cheese. Bake until the cheese is browned. Serve in gratin dish.

Broiled ham with pineapple

1 slice of ham, 1-inch thick

2 whole cloves

1 pineapple slice

1 tbsp. butter or margarine

1 maraschino cherry

Stick the cloves in the ham and broil in a hot greased skillet or broiler, 3 – 4 minutes on each side.

Melt the butter in a small saucepan and heat the pineapple slice.

To serve, place the ham on a heated plate and garnish with the pineapple slice and a maraschino cherry in the centre of the pineapple.

Ham with aurore sauce

2 tbsp. butter or margarine

1 tbsp. flour

¼ cup milk

2 tbsp. heavy cream

1 tbsp. tomato paste

Salt and pepper

Dash of cayenne pepper

1 slice of ham

1 tsp. chopped parsley

Melt 1 tablespoon butter in a small saucepan. Stir in the flour and blend in. Pour in the milk all at once and cook, stirring, until the sauce begins to thicken.

Add the cream and tomato paste, stirring briskly to blend in. Season with salt, pepper, and cayenne. Cook the ham in the remaining tablespoon of butter over low heat.

To serve, place the ham on a heated dish, pour sauce over, and sprinkle with chopped parsley.

Ham and potato casserole

1 tbsp. butter or margarine

1 tbsp. flour

$1/2$ cup milk

1 medium boiled potato, sliced

$2/3$ cup diced ham

1 tsp. chopped parsley

Preheat oven to 400°F.

Melt the butter in a small saucepan. Stir in the flour, add the milk all at once, and cook over low heat, stirring, until the sauce begins to thicken.

Place the slices of potato in the bottom of a buttered baking dish. Spoon some sauce over the potatoes, add the diced ham, and cover with the rest of the sauce. Sprinkle chopped parsley over.

Bake for 15 – 20 minutes. Serve in the baking dish.

Ham and rice

½ cup quick-cooking rice

2 tbsp. chopped onion

2 tbsp. butter or margarine

1 cup ham, cut into cubes

1 egg

Salt and pepper

1 tbsp. chopped parsley

Cook the rice according to the directions on the package.

Sauté the onion in a tablespoon of hot butter until tender.

Add the cubed ham and cook until golden brown.

Beat the eggs with salt and pepper to taste and cook in a small omelette pan.

When the omelette is cooked, cut into strips.

Mix the rice, onion, and ham. Sprinkle chopped parsley over and garnish with strips of omelette.

Liver with Madeira sauce

1 medium onion, sliced
2 tbsp. butter or margarine
1 or 2 slices pork liver
1 tbsp. flour
Salt and pepper
2 tbsp. beef bouillon
1 tbsp. tomato paste
1 tsp. prepared mustard
1 tbsp. Madeira
1 tsp. chopped parsley

Sauté the onion rings in hot butter, without letting them brown.
Remove from the pan and keep hot.
Dredge the liver in flour and season with salt and pepper.
Cook in the same pan as the onions.
When the liver is cooked, remove from the pan and keep hot.
Deglaze the pan with the beef bouillon, over high heat, scraping up the brown bits with a wooden spoon. Add the tomato paste, mustard, and Madeira. Salt and pepper to taste.
To serve, pour the sauce over the liver and garnish with onion rings and chopped parsley.

Liver with wine sauce

¼ lb. pork liver

2 tbsp. flour

1 tbsp. butter

1 tbsp. chopped shallot

¼ cup dry red wine

1 tsp. flour

1 tsp. butter or margarine

Salt and pepper

Dredge the liver in the flour and cook in hot butter over moderate heat.
Remove from the pan and keep hot.
Put the chopped shallot in the pan, add the wine, and bring to a rapid boil,
stirring. Let bubble for a few seconds. Then blend in the kneaded teaspoon of
flour and butter (*beurre manié*, see page 79). Season with salt and pepper.
Cook for a few minutes, stirring.
Pour the sauce over the liver and serve.

Pork chops milanese

2 pork chops

Salt and pepper

1 tbsp. flour

1 egg, lightly beaten

2 tbsp. breadcrumbs

1 tbsp. oil

2 tbsp. butter or margarine

½ cup elbow macaroni

1 tbsp. grated Parmesan cheese

1 tbsp. grated Gruyère cheese

Season the chops with salt and pepper and dredge lightly in flour. Dip in beaten egg and then in breadcrumbs.

Heat the oil and 1 tablespoon butter and cook the chops over moderate heat for 5 – 6 minutes on each side.

Meanwhile, cook the macaroni in salted, boiling water for about 10 minutes, or until tender. Drain well and return to saucepan. Stir in the remaining butter and the grated cheeses. Salt and pepper to taste. Keep hot.

When the chops are cooked, put the macaroni on a dish, place the chops on top, and spoon the pan juices over.

Pork chops with thyme

2 pork chops

1 small onion, chopped

2 tbsp. butter or margarine

1 medium carrot, cut in rounds

Salt and pepper

Pinch of thyme

1 egg yolk

1 tbsp. vinegar

Brown the chops and onion in hot butter. Add the carrot slices. Season with salt, pepper, and thyme.

Add hot water to cover and cook in covered pan for half an hour, or until the meat is tender. Add water during the cooking, if necessary, to prevent sticking. When the chops are cooked, remove from pan and keep hot.

Beat the egg yolk with the vinegar and pour carefully into the sauce in the pan, stirring. Continue to cook, stirring, without letting the sauce boil, until it thickens. Pour over the chops.

Pork chops in white wine

2 pork chops

Salt and pepper

3 tbsp. butter or margarine

1 small onion, finely chopped

¼ cup white wine

1 tsp. vinegar

¼ cup chicken bouillon

1 tsp. flour

½ tsp. mustard

2 sweet gherkins, cut into strips

Season the chops with salt and pepper, and brown in 1 tablespoon butter, over moderate heat, about 4 – 5 minutes on each side.
Sauté the onion in 1 tablespoon butter, without letting it brown.
Pour in the wine, vinegar, and bouillon and bring to a rapid boil.
Let bubble for 2 – 3 minutes while you knead the flour and remaining tablespoon of butter into a paste.* Beat into the sauce with a whisk. Add mustard and gherkins and continue cooking until sauce beings to thicken.
Place the chops on a warm dish and pour the sauce over.

* This kneaded flour-butter paste—*beurre manié*—is used as a thickening agent for sauces.

Scalloped pork chops

2 pork chops

Salt and pepper

1 tbsp. butter or margarine

2 tbsp. grated Gruyère cheese

¼ cup dry white wine

2 tbsp. whipping cream

1 tbsp. breadcrumbs

Preheat oven to 350°F.

Season the chops with salt and pepper and sauté in butter, over moderate heat, for 8 – 10 minutes. When browned on both sides, remove from pan and place in a buttered baking dish. Sprinkle with grated Gruyère cheese. Deglaze the pan with the wine, scraping up the brown bits with a wooden spoon. Add the cream and stir for a few seconds until the sauce is well blended. Pour the sauce over the chops, sprinkle breadcrumbs on top, and bake for 25 – 30 minutes, or until chops are tender.

Glazed sausages

1 tbsp. butter or margarine

1 tsp. prepared mustard

¼ cup maple syrup

2 smoked sausages

1 medium apple, peeled and quartered

1 cup cooked rice

Melt the butter in a small saucepan. Blend in the mustard and maple syrup.
Add the sausages and apple quarters, cover, and cook over low heat for
5 – 10 minutes.
Place the cooked rice on a heated plate, arrange the sausages and apples on
top, and pour the sauce over.

Lyonnaise blood pudding

1 small onion, sliced

2 tbsp. butter or margarine

Salt and pepper

2 thick slices of skinless blood sausage (about 5 – 6 oz.)

2 tbsp. lemon juice

½ tsp. chopped parsley

Brown the onion in 1 tablespoon butter. Season with salt and pepper and move to the edge of the pan. Add the remaining butter and cook the sausage for 2 – 3 minutes on each side.

When it is cooked, place the sausage on a heated plate and spoon the onions over.

Deglaze the pan with the lemon juice and pour the sauce over the onions. Sprinkle with chopped parsley.

Sausage casserole

3 pork sausages

1 tsp. butter or margarine

1/2 cup elbow macaroni

2 tbsp. chopped onion

1/4 cup green pepper, coarsely chopped

Salt and pepper

1/4 tsp. oregano

1/2 cup tomato sauce

2 tbsp. water

1/4 cup grated Parmesan cheese

Preheat oven to 400°F.

Brown the sausages in heated butter. Remove from the pan and cut into slices.

Cook the macaroni in salted, boiling water until tender. Drain, rinse in cold water, and drain again. Set aside.

Pour off the fat from the pan, except for 1 tablespoon. Add the onion and green pepper and sauté until tender. Season with salt, pepper, and oregano. Return the sausage slices to the pan, add the tomato sauce and water, and bring to a boil.

Reduce the heat and let simmer for 2 – 3 minutes. Add the cooked macaroni and one-half the Parmesan cheese, and mix well.

Put the mixture into a small baking dish, sprinkle with the remaining cheese, and bake until the top is delicately browned.

Sausage and macaroni casserole

½ cup elbow macaroni

2 smoked sausages, sliced

2 tbsp. chopped onion

2 tbsp. green pepper, diced

1 tbsp. butter or margarine

½ cup tomato sauce

¼ cup water

¼ tsp. oregano

Salt and pepper to taste

2 tbsp. grated mozzarella cheese

3 – 4 small slices mozzarella cheese

Preheat oven to 500°F.

Cook the macaroni in salted, boiling water until tender, about 10 – 15 minutes. Drain well and place in a well-buttered gratin dish.

Brown the sausages with the onion and green pepper in hot butter. Add the tomato sauce, water, oregano, salt, and pepper and simmer for 2 – 3 minutes over moderate heat, stirring frequently. Add the grated cheese and stir until melted.

Pour the mixture over the macaroni and arrange the slices of mozzarella on top. Bake until crusty and delicately browned. Serve in the gratin dish.

Sausages and sauerkraut

2 medium potatoes

2 tbsp. milk

2 tbsp. butter or margarine

Salt and pepper to taste

1 cup sauerkraut, drained

1 tbsp. chopped shallot

3 pork sausages

1 tbsp. grated Parmesan cheese

Preheat oven to 400°F.

Cook the potatoes in salted, boiling water until tender. Drain and mash with the milk, 1 tablespoon butter, and salt and pepper.

Mix the sauerkraut and shallot and place in a baking dish.

Brown the sausages in the remaining tablespoon of butter and place them on top of the sauerkraut.

Spread the mashed potatoes over and sprinkle with grated cheese.

Bake until delicately browned.

Sausages in white wine

1 tbsp. butter or margarine

1 tbsp. flour

3 – 4 sausages

1 tbsp. oil

⅓ cup dry white wine

1 tsp. chopped tarragon

Salt and pepper to taste

Knead the butter and flour into a smooth paste. Set aside.

Cook the sausages in hot oil, over low heat, until well-browned. Remove from the pan and keep hot.

Deglaze the pan with the white wine, scraping up the brown bits from the bottom.

Add the tarragon, salt, and pepper.

Thicken the sauce by blending in the butter-flour paste (*beurre manié*, see page 79).

Pour the sauce over the sausages.

Baked veal scallop

1 veal scallop

Salt and pepper

1 tbsp. oil

½ cup chopped onion

1 tbsp. butter or margarine

2 tbsp. dry white wine

¼ cup breadcrumbs

1 tbsp. grated Parmesan cheese

1 tsp. melted butter

Preheat oven to 350°F.

Season the veal scallop with salt and pepper and brown in hot oil.

Place the chopped onion in a 9-inch pie plate and dot with butter. Lay the scallop on the onions and sprinkle wine over.

Mix the breadcrumbs, cheese, and melted butter and sprinkle over the scallop.

Bake for about 30 minutes, or until the meat is tender.

Gourmet veal scallop

¼ cup sliced mushrooms
2 tbsp. butter or margarine
1 slice of Gruyère cheese, the same size as the scallop
1 medium veal scallop
Salt and pepper
1 tbsp. cognac
2 tbsp. hot water
2 tbsp. port
1 tsp. tomato paste
Dash of cayenne pepper
1 tsp. cornstarch
2 tbsp. heavy cream
2 tbsp. breadcrumbs

Preheat oven to 500°F.

Sauté the mushrooms in 1 tablespoon butter, then place in a gratin or baking dish and cover with the cheese slice.

Season the scallop with salt and pepper and cook in 1 tablespoon butter, over moderate heat, for 4 – 5 minutes on each side, or until tender. Sprinkle the scallop with the cognac and ignite with a lighted match. When the flames die down, place the scallop on top of the cheese in the gratin dish. Deglaze the pan with hot water and port, scraping the bottom of the pan with a wooden spoon. Add the tomato paste, cayenne pepper, and the cornstarch blended with the cream. Cook, stirring, until the sauce thickens.

Pour the sauce over the scallop, sprinkle breadcrumbs over, and dot with butter.

Bake in hot oven until breadcrumbs are golden brown.

Liver and bacon

2 slices bacon

2 tbsp. butter or margarine

4 – 6 oz. calves' liver

2 tbsp. flour

1 shallot, chopped

Salt and pepper

1/2 tsp. prepared mustard

1/3 cup dry white wine

Fry the bacon in 1 tablespoon butter. Remove from pan and keep hot.
Dredge the liver lightly in flour and fry, with the shallot, in the bacon pan.
Season with salt and pepper and transfer to a heated plate. Lay the bacon
slices over the liver.

Mix the mustard and wine and pour into the pan, scraping the bottom of the
pan to deglaze it. Swirl in the rest of the butter and pour the sauce over the
liver and bacon.

Liver and onions

1 small onion, thinly sliced

2 tbsp. butter or margarine

1 tsp. sugar

Salt and pepper

1 tbsp. flour

4 – 6 oz. calves' liver

¼ cup heavy cream

Sauté the onion in hot butter. Season with sugar, salt, and pepper and cook until brown. Push to one side of the pan.

Dredge the liver lightly in flour and cook, with the onions, for 3 – 4 minutes on each side, until done.

Remove from the pan and keep hot.

Deglaze the pan with the cream and pour the sauce over the liver and onions.

Pan-fried veal scallop

1 tbsp. butter or margarine

1 tsp. oil

1 medium veal scallop

Salt and pepper

¼ cup chicken bouillon

2 tbsp. dry white wine

Heat the butter and oil in a frying pan and cook the scallop for 4 – 5 minutes on each side. Season with salt and pepper. Remove the scallop and keep hot. Pour in the chicken bouillon and wine and deglaze the pan, scraping the bottom vigorously. Return the scallop to the pan and cook for 2 minutes over low heat, being careful not to let the sauce boil.

Veal chop and vegetables

½ cup cut green beans

½ cup carrots, cut into rounds

2 small whole onions

1 veal chop

1 tbsp. butter or margarine

Salt and pepper

Cook the beans and carrots in salted, boiling water.

Drain well and set aside.

Sauté the onions and the veal chop in hot butter.

Add the vegetables, season with salt and pepper, and continue cooking over moderate heat until the meat is tender.

Veal scallop with cream sauce

1 veal scallop

1 tbsp. butter or margarine

$\frac{1}{4}$ cup sliced mushrooms

Salt and pepper to taste

$\frac{1}{3}$ cup cream

Dash of cayenne pepper

Sauté the veal scallop on both sides in hot butter.

Add the mushrooms, salt, and pepper and continue cooking, over moderate heat, until the meat is tender.

Remove the scallop and keep hot.

Pour the cream into the saucepan and stir briskly, scraping the bottom to deglaze.

Add the cayenne pepper. Place the scallop on a heated plate and pour the sauce over.

Veal scallop in white wine

1 veal scallop

1 tbsp. flour

1 tbsp. butter or margarine

Salt and pepper

⅓ cup mushrooms, sliced

½ tsp. instant chicken bouillon base

½ cup dry white wine

1 tsp. chopped parsley

Dredge the scallop lightly in flour and brown in hot butter, 4 – 5 minutes on each side. Season with salt and pepper and remove from pan.

Sauté the mushrooms in the same pan for 2 – 3 minutes, stirring.

Mix the chicken bouillon base with the wine, pour into the pan, and bring to a rapid boil, stirring. Reduce heat, return the scallop to the pan, cover, and continue cooking for 25 – 30 minutes, or until the meat is tender.

Sprinkle chopped parsley.

Wiener schnitzel

1 veal scallop

Salt and pepper

1 egg, beaten

2 tbsp. breadcrumbs

2 tbsp. butter or margarine

1 slice lemon

Sprig of fresh parsley

Season the scallop with salt and pepper.

Dip in beaten egg, then in breadcrumbs.

Sauté on both sides in hot butter.

When cooked, transfer to heated plate and garnish with lemon slice and parsley.

Chicken

Baked chicken

1 chicken breast or thigh

¼ cup chopped onion

¼ cup sliced mushrooms

1 tbsp. butter or margarine

½ cup cream of chicken soup

¼ cup apple juice

1 tsp. Worcestershire sauce

1 clove garlic, crushed

Salt and pepper to taste

Paprika

Preheat oven to 350°F.

Place the chicken in a lightly buttered baking dish.

Sauté the onion and mushrooms in hot butter and spread on top of the chicken.

Mix the undiluted chicken soup, apple juice, Worcestershire sauce, garlic, salt, and pepper and pour over the chicken.

Bake for about one hour, basting occasionally.

When ready to serve, sprinkle with paprika.

Serve with rice and almonds (see page 227).

Breaded chicken

¼ cup flour

1 tbsp. breadcrumbs

½ tsp. paprika

Salt and pepper to taste

1 chicken part

2 tbsp. oil

Mix the flour, breadcrumbs, paprika, salt, and pepper.

Dredge the chicken in this mixture and brown in hot oil.

Cover and cook, over low heat, until tender, about 30 – 35 minutes.

Uncover and continue cooking 5 – 10 minutes longer.

Chicken Catalina

1 chicken breast or thigh

2 tbsp. butter or margarine

Salt and pepper

1/4 tsp. paprika

1/3 cup chopped onion

1/4 cup chopped celery

1/2 cup Catalina salad dressing

1/2 cup canned pineapple chunks, drained

1/2 cup quick-cooking rice

1/2 cup pineapple juice

Brown the chicken in hot butter. Season with salt, pepper, and paprika.
Add the onion, celery, and salad dressing. Cover and cook over moderate
heat until tender, about 30 – 40 minutes.
Add the pineapple chunks and heat for a few minutes.
Cook the rice according to directions on the package, substituting juice from
the canned pineapple for the water. Serve with the chicken.

Chicken with garlic

1 tbsp. oil

2 tbsp. flour

Salt and pepper to taste

Pinch of paprika

1 chicken breast or thigh

¼ cup chicken bouillon

1 tbsp. apple juice

1 clove garlic, crushed

Preheat oven to 375°F.

Mix the flour, salt, pepper, and paprika. Dredge the chicken in the seasoned flour.

Cook the chicken in hot oil, over moderate heat, until browned on all sides. Place in a baking dish.

Mix the bouillon, apple juice, and garlic and pour over chicken. Bake, covered, for about one hour, basting occasionally.

Chicken with mushrooms

1 chicken breast or thigh
¼ tsp. paprika
½ cup chicken bouillon
¼ cup dry white wine
Pinch of curry powder
1 tbsp. grated onion
Salt and pepper to taste
1 tbsp. butter or margarine
½ cup sliced mushrooms
1 tsp. flour

Preheat oven to 350°F.

Place the chicken in a baking dish and sprinkle with paprika.

Add the bouillon, wine, curry powder, grated onion, salt, and pepper.

Bake, covered, for one hour. Remove cover during the last 15 minutes, to let the chicken brown.

Sauté the mushrooms in hot butter. Set aside.

When the chicken is cooked, remove from baking dish and keep hot.

Bring the cooking juices in the baking dish to a boil. Add the flour mixed with a little cold water and cook, stirring, until the sauce begins to thicken. Add the mushrooms and heat for a few minutes.

Pour the sauce over the chicken.

Chicken with onions

1 chicken breast or thigh

1 tbsp. butter or margarine

¼ cup finely chopped onion

1 tsp. flour

½ cup chicken bouillon

Salt and pepper

⅓ cup sliced mushrooms

4 small canned onions, drained

Brown the chicken in hot butter. Add the onion and cook for a minute.
Stir in the flour mixed with the bouillon. Season with salt and pepper.
Cover and cook over low heat for about 45 minutes.
Five minutes before the end of the cooking period, add the mushrooms and
canned onions.

Chicken à l'orange

1 chicken breast or thigh

Pinch of curry powder

¼ cup orange juice

1 tbsp. honey

2 tsp. prepared mustard

2 tsp. cornstarch

1 tbsp. cold water

2 – 3 slices peeled orange

Preheat oven to 375°F.

Place the chicken in a baking dish and sprinkle with curry powder.

Heat the orange juice, honey, and mustard in a small saucepan, stirring, until the mixture comes to a gentle boil.

Pour over the chicken. Bake for 30 minutes.

Turn the chicken over and continue cooking for 10 – 15 minutes, or until tender. Remove from baking dish and keep hot.

Mix the cornstarch and water and pour into the baking dish.

Cook over low heat, stirring, until the sauce thickens. Add the orange slices and heat for a minute.

Pour the sauce over the chicken.

Chicken supreme

1 chicken breast

2 tbsp. butter or margarine

¼ cup finely chopped onion

1 tsp. flour

¼ cup chicken bouillon

¼ cup whipping cream

1 tsp. Worcestershire sauce

Salt and pepper to taste

Chopped parsley

Cook the chicken breast in 1 tablespoon hot butter. When browned on all sides, reduce heat and continue cooking, covered, for about 45 minutes, or until tender.

Melt the remaining tablespoon of butter in a small saucepan and cook the onions over low heat until soft but not browned.

Sprinkle flour over and stir in. Add the bouillon, cream, Worcestershire sauce, salt, and pepper and bring to a boil, stirring constantly.

When the chicken is cooked, drain the fat off, pour the sauce over, and let simmer for a few minutes.

Sprinkle with chopped parsley.

Fried chicken with tomato sauce

2 tbsp. flour

Salt and pepper to taste

1 chicken breast or thigh

1 tbsp. oil

¼ cup chopped onion

¼ cup tomato sauce

¼ cup water

1 tbsp. vinegar

1 tbsp. brown sugar

½ tsp. Worcestershire sauce

Mix the flour, salt, and pepper. Dredge the chicken in the seasoned flour and brown in hot oil with the chopped onion.
Mix the remaining ingredients and pour over the chicken. Cover and cook 30 – 40 minutes, or until tender, basting frequently.

Sautéed chicken with mushrooms

1 tbsp. oil
1 tbsp. butter or margarine
1 chicken breast or thigh
½ cup sliced mushrooms
1 clove garlic, crushed
Salt and pepper to taste
1 shallot, chopped
½ cup dry white wine
1 tbsp. butter or margarine
1 tbsp. flour

Heat the oil and butter and brown the chicken on all sides. Add the mushrooms, parsley, garlic, salt, and pepper and continue cooking until the chicken is tender. Remove the chicken and mushrooms from the pan and keep hot.

Sauté the chopped shallot quickly over high heat, add the wine, and cook for about a minute, until the liquid is reduced. Thicken the sauce by stirring in the *beurre manié* (butter—flour paste, see page 79).

Place the chicken and mushrooms on a heated plate and pour the sauce over.

Fish and shellfish

Baked fish and tomato with rice

1 medium tomato

1/3 cup grated Cheddar cheese

4 – 6 oz. fish fillet

Salt and pepper

1/4 cup sliced mushrooms

2 tbsp. butter or margarine

1/4 cup quick-cooking rice

Chopped parsley

Preheat oven to 350°F.

Cut the tomato in two, scoop out the pulp, and fill each half with the grated cheese.

Place the fish fillet in a buttered baking dish. Season with salt and pepper.

Place a tomato half on each side of the fillet. Bake for about 20 – 25 minutes, or until the fish flakes easily with a fork.

Meanwhile, brown the mushrooms in 1 tablespoon butter and keep hot.

Cook the rice according to the directions on the package. Add the remaining tablespoon of butter and the mushrooms.

To serve, spoon the rice onto a heated plate, place the fish on top, garnish with the tomato halves, and sprinkle parsley over.

Broiled salmon

2 tbsp. oil
1 tbsp. vinegar
1 tsp. lemon juice
Salt and pepper to taste
¼ tsp. rosemary
1 salmon steak, ¾-inch thick

Mix the oil, vinegar, lemon juice, salt, pepper, and rosemary.

Marinate the salmon in this mixture for about half an hour at room temperature.

Broil the salmon on a hot, well-greased broiler rack for 6 – 7 minutes, brushing occasionally with the marinade.

Turn the steak and cook the other side for 4 – 5 minutes, continuing to brush with the marinade.

Cod fillet with green pepper

¼ cup green pepper, coarsely chopped

2 tbsp. oil

1 cod fillet

½ cup tomato sauce

1 tbsp. lemon juice

1 tsp. Worcestershire sauce

Salt and pepper to taste

Stir-fry the green pepper in hot oil for 2 – 3 minutes.

Move it to one side of the pan and add the cod fillet.

When the fish is browned on both sides, add the remaining ingredients. Cover and cook over low heat for 5 minutes, or until the fish flakes easily with a fork.

To use the rest of the canned tomato sauce, see the following recipes:
Fried chicken, page 107
Haddock with tomato sauce, page 120
Baked rigatoni, page 159

Creamed haddock in scallop shell

2 tbsp. finely chopped onion

¼ cup sliced mushrooms

3 tbsp. butter or margarine

⅔ cup haddock, flaked

1 tbsp. flour

¾ cup milk

1 clove garlic, crushed

1 tsp. chopped parsley

Salt and pepper

Pinch of nutmeg

1 tbsp. breadcrumbs

Preheat oven to 500°F.

Sauté the onion and mushrooms in 2 tablespoons butter. Add the fish and cook, stirring, for 1 – 2 minutes. Remove from heat and set aside.

Melt the remaining tablespoon of butter. Stir in the flour. Pour in the milk all at once and cook, stirring, until the sauce begins to thicken.

Add the fish mixture, stirring gently. Season with garlic, parsley, salt, pepper, and nutmeg.

Turn the mixture into a scallop shell. Sprinkle with breadcrumbs and dot with butter.

Bake for about 10 minutes.

Creamed salmon

1 tbsp. butter or margarine

1 tbsp. flour

1 cup milk

Salt and pepper

1 can salmon (7¾ oz.)

¼ cup canned peas, drained

2 stuffed olives, sliced

1 tsp. lemon juice

¼ tsp. dried dill

1 English muffin, toasted

1 sprig parsley

Melt the butter in a pan. When the foam subsides, stir in the flour.

Add the milk all at once, season with salt and pepper, and cook, stirring, until the sauce begins to bubble.

Add the salmon, peas, olives, lemon juice, and dill, and heat for 4 – 5 minutes.

Place the toasted muffin on a plate and spoon the salmon mixture over.

Garnish with a sprig of parsley.

To use the rest of the canned peas, see the following recipes:
Minted peas, page 150
Green peas and onions, page 147

Fillet of sole with asparagus

4 asparagus spears, cooked

2 tbsp. mayonnaise

1 tbsp. sweet relish

1 fillet of sole

1 tbsp. chili sauce

Preheat oven to 350°F.

Lay the asparagus spears in a lightly buttered baking dish.

Mix the mayonnaise and relish and spoon over the asparagus. Place the fish fillet on top and spoon chili sauce over.

Bake for 30 – 35 minutes, or until the fish flakes easily with a fork.

Fish fillet amandine

| 1 fish fillet (sole, haddock, or cod) |
| 1 fish fillet (sole, haddock, or cod) |
| Salt and pepper |
| 2 tbsp. flour |
| 2 tbsp. oil |
| ¼ cup whipping cream |
| 1 tbsp. lemon juice |
| Pinch of cayenne pepper |
| 1 tbsp. slivered almonds, toasted |

Season the fish fillet with salt and pepper, dredge lightly in flour, and brown in hot oil, 2 – 3 minutes on each side. Remove from the pan and keep hot.
Pour off the fat from the pan, add the cream, and cook gently, stirring.
Add the lemon juice and season with salt, pepper, and cayenne.
Pour the sauce over the fish, garnish with the toasted almonds, and serve.

Fish fillet with apple and onion sauce

2 tbsp. flour

Curry powder

Salt and pepper

4 – 6 oz. fillet of sole, haddock, or cod

2 tbsp. butter or margarine

¼ cup chopped onion

¼ cup apple, peeled and grated

1 tsp. vinegar

½ cup milk

Pinch of cayenne pepper

Mix 1 tablespoon flour, a pinch of curry powder, salt, and pepper. Cut the fillet into bite-sized pieces, dredge in the seasoned flour, and cook in 1 tablespoon hot butter. Remove and keep hot.

Brown the onion in the remaining tablespoon of butter. Add the apple and one-quarter teaspoon curry powder mixed with the vinegar. Stir in the remaining tablespoon flour and cook for about one minute. Gradually pour in the milk, stirring, and cook until the sauce thickens.

Pour over the fish and sprinkle with cayenne pepper.

Haddock with tomato sauce

¼ cup chopped onion

¼ cup chopped celery

1 tbsp. chopped parsley

1 haddock fillet

2 tsp. oil

Salt and pepper

¼ tsp. paprika

⅓ cup canned tomato sauce

Preheat oven to 350°F.

Mix the onion, celery, and parsley and sprinkle on the bottom of a baking dish.

Place the fish on this mixture and brush with the oil. Season with salt, pepper, and paprika and bake for 5 minutes.

Pour the tomato sauce over and continue baking 10 minutes longer, or until the fish flakes easily with a fork.

Suggestions for using the rest of the tomato sauce:

Fried chicken, page 107

Cod fillet with green pepper, page 114

Baked rigatoni, page 159

Herbed haddock

1 tbsp. butter or margarine

1 tbsp. flour

½ cup milk

Salt and pepper

¼ tsp. oregano

1 tsp. minced chives

1 haddock fillet

Pinch of paprika

Preheat the oven to 350°F.

Melt the butter in a small saucepan. When the foam subsides, stir in the flour.
Pour the milk in all at once and cook over low heat, stirring, until the sauce
begins to thicken. Season with salt, pepper, oregano, and chives.
Place the fish fillet in a buttered baking dish and pour the sauce over.
Sprinkle lightly with paprika and bake for 30 – 35 minutes.

Salmon steak with basil

2 tbsp. butter or margarine, melted

1 tbsp. lemon juice

1 salmon steak

Salt and pepper

¼ tsp. basil

1 lemon wedge

1 sprig parsley

Preheat oven to 400°F.

Mix the melted butter and lemon juice and turn the salmon in the mixture until the liquid is absorbed.

Place the salmon in a buttered baking dish. Season with salt, pepper, and basil. Bake 25 minutes, or until the salmon flakes easily with a fork.

Transfer the salmon to a heated plate and garnish with the lemon wedge and parsley.

Shrimp with spinach rice

½ cup cream of shrimp soup

¼ cup table cream

1 tbsp. grated onion

1 tsp. parsley

¼ tsp. curry powder

1 cup shrimp, cooked

⅓ cup quick-cooking rice

¼ cup cooked spinach, finely chopped

1 tbsp. grated onion

2 tsp. butter or margarine

Mix the shrimp soup, cream, onion, parsley, and curry powder in a small saucepan and cook over low heat until the mixture begins to bubble.
Add the shrimp and simmer over very low heat. Cook the rice according to the directions on the package. Add the remaining ingredients to the rice and serve with the shrimp sauce.

The rest of the canned shrimp soup can be used as a sauce with fried fish or with vegetable dishes, or as soup, sprinkled with dried dill.

Eggs

Baked egg with chives

1 egg
1 tbsp. whipping cream
1 tsp. chopped chives
Salt and pepper

Preheat oven to 350°F.

Break the egg into a small, well buttered custard dish.

Beat the cream lightly with a fork, add the chives and salt and pepper to taste, and pour over the egg.

Place the dish in a pan of hot water and bake for 8 – 10 minutes, or until the white is set but the yolk is still soft.

Serve with toast and coffee for breakfast.

Baked mushroom omelette

¼ cup sliced mushrooms

2 tbsp. butter or margarine

1 tbsp. flour

½ cup milk

2 tbsp. grated Gruyère cheese

Salt and pepper to taste

2 eggs

Preheat oven to 500°F.

Sauté the mushrooms in 1 tablespoon of hot butter. Set aside.

Melt the remaining tablespoon of butter in a small pan. Stir in the flour. Add the milk and cook, stirring, until the mixture begins to thicken.

Remove from heat, add 1 tablespoon grated cheese, salt and pepper, and stir until the cheese is melted.

Beat the eggs, season with salt and pepper, and pour over the mushrooms. Cook until the bottom is browned. Roll the omelette and slide into a lightly buttered gratin dish. Pour the sauce over, sprinkle with the remaining cheese, and bake until the top is golden brown.

Egg Lorraine

2 slices bacon

1 egg

2 tbsp. whipping cream

Salt and pepper to taste

1 slice bread, toasted

1 thin slice Gruyère cheese

Preheat oven to 350°F.

Fry the bacon slices, drain on paper towelling, and set aside.

Beat the egg with the cream, salt, and pepper.

Place the toast in a small, buttered baking dish. Arrange the cheese and bacon slices on top. Pour the egg mixture over.

Bake about 10 minutes.

Omelette American style

2 eggs

2 tbsp. sour cream

Salt and pepper to taste

2 tbsp. tomato, peeled and chopped

1 small shallot, chopped

2 tbsp. grated Cheddar cheese

Preheat oven to 325°F.

Beat the eggs with the sour cream, salt, and pepper.

Add the tomato, shallot, and cheese.

Pour into a small, buttered pie plate and bake 15 – 20 minutes.

Scrambled eggs Italian style

1 tbsp. butter or margarine

2 tbsp. chopped green pepper

2 tbsp. thinly sliced mushrooms

1 shallot, chopped

2 tbsp. diced pepperoni sausage

2 eggs

2 tbsp. milk

Salt and pepper to taste

Brown the green pepper, mushrooms, and shallot in hot butter until tender. Add the diced pepperoni sausage. Beat the eggs with the milk, salt, and pepper and pour into the pepperoni mixture. Cook, stirring, over low heat. Serve with a small green salad.

Tomato stuffed with egg

1 large tomato

1 egg

1 tbsp. grated Gruyère cheese

Salt and pepper

½ tsp. chopped chives

1 cup finely chopped lettuce

1 tbsp. mayonnaise

Preheat oven to 350°F.

Cut the top off the tomato, scoop out the pulp, and season the inside with salt and pepper. Place in a small custard dish and bake for two minutes.

Remove from the oven and carefully break an egg into the tomato. Sprinkle with the cheese and chives. Return to the oven for 10 minutes.

Place the chopped lettuce in a salad bowl. Mix the mayonnaise with the tomato pulp and pour over. Season with salt and pepper.

Serve the stuffed tomato in the custard dish.

Tuna fish omelette

2 tbsp. butter or margarine

2 tbsp. chopped shallot

½ cup canned tuna, drained

1 egg

1 tbsp. cream

Salt and pepper to taste

Brown the shallot in 1 tablespoon butter.

Add the tuna fish and heat gently for a minute or two. Set aside.

Beat the egg with the cream, salt, and pepper. Melt the remaining tablespoon of butter in a frying pan. Pour the beaten egg into the pan and cook over low heat. When the omelette is set on the bottom but still moist on top, place the tuna fish mixture on one half of the omelette and fold the other half over.

Turn onto a heated plate and serve.

Vegetables

Asparagus and almonds

4 – 5 asparagus spears

1 tbsp. butter or margarine

1 tbsp. slivered almonds

Salt

1 tsp. lemon juice

Cook the asparagus in salted, boiling water for about 15 minutes, or just until tender. Drain and keep hot.

Sauté the slivered almonds in hot butter, stirring constantly. Remove from heat, season with salt, add the lemon juice, and pour over asparagus.

Asparagus au gratin

6 asparagus tips

1 hard-cooked egg, chopped

2 tbsp. grated Gruyère cheese

¼ cup whipping cream

Salt and pepper

Preheat oven to 500°F.

Cook the asparagus in salted, boiling water for about 15 minutes, or just until tender. Drain well and place in a buttered gratin dish.

Mix the chopped egg, grated cheese, and cream. Season with salt and pepper.

Spread the mixture over the asparagus and bake till golden brown.

Asparagus with tomato sauce

2 tbsp. mayonnaise

1 tsp. lemon juice

Salt and pepper to taste

1 small tomato, peeled and finely chopped

4 freshly cooked asparagus spears

Heat the mayonnaise, lemon juice, salt, pepper, and tomato over low heat.
Spoon the sauce over the hot asparagus.

Broccoli with mustard sauce

5 oz. broccoli, fresh or frozen

1 tbsp. sour cream

1 tbsp. mayonnaise

1/4 tsp. prepared mustard

1/2 tsp. lemon juice

Pinch of paprika

Cook the fresh broccoli in salted, boiling water until tender. (If using frozen broccoli, follow directions on the package.)

Heat the sour cream, mayonnaise, mustard, and lemon juice over very low heat.

When the broccoli is cooked, drain, spoon mustard sauce over, sprinkle lightly with paprika, and serve.

Brussels sprouts with cashew nuts

1 cup frozen Brussels sprouts

2 tbsp. cashew nuts

2 tbsp. butter or margarine

Cook the Brussels sprouts according to directions on the package. Drain well. Add the nuts and butter and heat slowly, stirring gently, until sprouts are coated with butter.

Cauliflower with butter

1 cup cauliflower flowerets

2 tbsp. butter or margarine, melted

1 tsp. chopped parsley

Cook the cauliflower in salted, boiling water for 10 – 15 minutes, or until tender.

Drain well and place in a heated dish. Drizzle melted butter over and sprinkle with chopped parsley.

Cauliflower with nutmeg

1 cup cauliflower flowerets

2 tbsp. soft butter or margarine

¼ tsp. nutmeg

Cook the cauliflower in salted, boiling water for 10 – 15 minutes, or just until tender. Drain well and place in a heated dish.
Blend the butter and nutmeg and spread over the cauliflower.

Creamed carrots

1 tbsp. oil

1 tbsp. butter or margarine

1 cup carrots, thinly sliced

Salt and pepper

1 tbsp. flour

½ cup warm water

Pinch of nutmeg

2 tbsp. cream

1 tsp. chopped parsley

Brown the sliced carrots in heated oil and butter for 2 – 3 minutes over moderate heat. Season with salt and pepper.

Sprinkle flour over and mix well. Add the water and nutmeg and blend in. Cover and cook for 15 – 20 minutes, stirring occasionally.

Add the cream and chopped parsley and serve immediately.

Green bean salad

2 tbsp. oil

1 tsp. vinegar

Salt and pepper to taste

1 tbsp. chopped shallot

6 oz. cooked green beans

1 hard-cooked egg, sliced

½ tsp. chopped parsley

½ tsp. chopped chives

Mix the oil, vinegar, salt, pepper, and chopped shallot and pour over the beans.

Garnish with egg slices and sprinkle with parsley and chives.

Green beans with almonds

2 tbsp. slivered almonds

1 tbsp. butter or margarine

1 cup green beans, cooked

Sauté the almonds in hot butter. Add the beans and heat for a few minutes.

Green peas and onions

1 tbsp. butter or margarine

¼ cup chopped onions

½ cup canned green peas, drained

Salt and pepper to taste

Sauté the onions in hot butter until golden. Add the peas, salt, and pepper and cook gently until the peas are heated through.

Herb carrots

2 tbsp. butter or margarine

1 tbsp. water

½ tsp. sugar

1 cup carrots, cut up

Salt and pepper

1 tsp. chopped parsley

1 tsp. tarragon

Melt the butter and blend in the sugar and water. Add the carrots and cook, covered, over low heat for 15 – 20 minutes, or until tender.
Season with salt and pepper and sprinkle with parsley and tarragon.

Herb turnips

1 cup turnip, cut in cubes

½ tsp. sugar

1 tbsp. butter or margarine

1 small onion, sliced

Salt and pepper to taste

1 tsp. chopped parsley

1 tsp. tarragon

Cook the turnip in sugared, boiling water until tender but not too soft. Drain well.

Sauté the onion slices in hot butter for 4 – 5 minutes.

Add the turnip and seasonings and cook 2 – 3 minutes longer, stirring occasionally.

Minted peas

1 tbsp. butter or margarine

1 tbsp. mint jelly

½ cup canned green peas, drained

1 tbsp. liquid from canned peas

Salt and pepper

Melt the butter and mint jelly in a small saucepan.

Add the peas and liquid. Season with salt and pepper and cook over low heat until the peas are heated through.

Parslied new potatoes

2 small new potatoes

2 tbsp. butter or margarine

1 tsp. chopped parsley

1 tsp. lemon juice

Salt and pepper to taste

Scrub the potatoes and cook in salted, boiling water for 10 – 15 minutes, or until tender. Drain, peel, and keep hot.

Melt the butter in a small saucepan. Add the parsley, lemon juice, salt, and pepper and pour over the potatoes.

Potatoes with mustard sauce

1 medium potato, peeled and sliced

1 tbsp. butter or margarine

¼ cup hot water

2 tbsp. cream

1 tsp. Dijon mustard

Salt and pepper

½ tsp. chopped chervil

Melt the butter in a frying pan and sauté the potato slices, over moderately high heat, until golden brown.

Add the hot water, reduce heat, cover, and cook 5 – 10 minutes, or until tender.

Blend the cream, mustard, salt, and pepper and simmer over very low heat, stirring.

Spoon the mustard sauce over the potatoes and sprinkle with the chopped chervil.

Sautéed turnip

1 cup turnip, cut in 1-inch cubes

Sugar

1 tbsp. butter or margarine

Salt and pepper

1 clove crushed garlic

1 tsp. chopped parsley

Cook the turnip in boiling water sweetened with a little sugar for 10 – 15 minutes, or until tender but not too soft.

Drain well and sauté in hot butter over moderately high heat for 5 minutes. Season with salt and pepper. Add the garlic and chopped parsley and continue cooking for a few minutes longer, stirring occasionally to prevent sticking.

Wax beans with chili sauce

1 cup cut wax beans
¼ cup chopped celery
1 tbsp. butter or margarine
2 tbsp. chicken bouillon
1 tbsp. chili sauce

Cook the beans in salted, boiling water until tender. Drain.

Sauté the celery in hot butter for about 5 minutes.

Add the chicken bouillon and bring to a boil.

Add the chili sauce and cooked beans. Heat for a few minutes, stirring gently.

Wax beans with tarragon

2 tbsp. butter or margarine

1 cup canned wax beans, drained

1 tbsp. chopped pimento

Salt and pepper to taste

½ tsp. tarragon

Melt the butter. When the foam subsides, add the remaining ingredients and heat slowly, stirring gently.

Pastas

Baked rigatoni

1½ cups rigatoni

Salt and pepper

2 tbsp. butter or margarine

1 smoked sausage, sliced

1 tbsp. flour

¾ cup milk

2 tbsp. grated Gruyère cheese

⅓ cup canned tomato sauce

4 – 5 slices pepperoni sausage

4 – 5 small slices mozzarella cheese

Preheat oven to 500°F.

Cook the rigatoni in salted, boiling water until tender.

Rinse and drain well. Season with salt and pepper.

Add 1 tablespoon butter and smoked sausage slices and mix well. Turn into a buttered baking dish.

Melt the remaining tablespoon butter. Stir in the flour, add the milk, and cook, stirring, until the sauce begins to thicken. Remove from heat, add the Gruyère cheese, and stir until completely melted. Cover the rigatoni with the cheese sauce and pour the tomato sauce over. Arrange pepperoni and mozzarella cheese slices on top and bake until golden brown.

The rest of the tomato sauce can be used in the following recipes:

Fried chicken with tomato sauce, page 107
Cod fillet with green pepper, page 114
Haddock with tomato sauce, page 120

Herbed noodles

4 – 6 oz. noodles

2 tbsp. butter or margarine

¼ tsp. rosemary

⅛ tsp. marjoram

2 tsp. parsley

Cook the noodles in salted, boiling water.

Rinse and drain well. Return to saucepan, add butter and herbs, and heat, stirring.

Macaroni and cheese with bacon

½ cup cut macaroni

2 slices bacon

¼ cup chopped onion

¼ cup grated Cheddar cheese

¼ cup canned tomato soup

¼ cup milk

Preheat oven to 375°F.

Cook the macaroni in salted, boiling water for 10 minutes. Drain, rinse, and set aside.

Fry the bacon until crisp, drain, and crumble.

Sauté the onion in 1 tablespoon bacon fat for 2 – 3 minutes.

Mix the macaroni, bacon, onion, cheese, soup, and milk. Turn into a buttered baking dish and bake for 10 – 15 minutes, until the cheese is melted and the macaroni heated.

Dilute the rest of the canned soup with a little milk and heat slowly. Sprinkle with a pinch of chopped chives or parsley and serve.

Meat and macaroni

¼ lb. minced beef

½ cup cut macaroni

2 tbsp. chopped onion

2 tbsp. green pepper, chopped

1 tbsp. oil

1 cup tomato juice

1 clove garlic, crushed

1 tsp. Worcestershire sauce

Salt and pepper to taste

Cook the meat, macaroni, onion, and pepper in hot oil for about 5 minutes, stirring frequently.

Add the tomato juice, garlic, Worcestershire sauce, salt, and pepper.

Cover and cook about 20 minutes, or until the macaroni is tender, stirring occasionally.

Refrigerate the rest of the tomato juice until the next day. With a squeeze of lemon juice, a pinch of basil, and a little salt and pepper, it's a refreshing appetizer.

Salads and cold plates

Artichoke salad

1 – 2 lettuce leaves

²/₃ cup marinated artichoke hearts, drained

1 onion slice, separated into rings

2 stuffed olives, sliced

1 tbsp. salad oil

1 tsp. vinegar

Salt and pepper

Place the artichoke hearts, onion rings, and olives on a bed of lettuce leaves.
Blend the oil, vinegar, salt, and pepper and pour over.
Serve very cold.

Chicken salad

1 cup cooked chicken, diced

1 small endive, chopped

¼ cup apple, diced

1 tbsp. chopped nuts

2 tbsp. finely chopped celery

2 tbsp. lemon juice

Salt and pepper

1 tsp. prepared mustard

¼ cup mayonnaise

Combine the first five ingredients in a small salad bowl. Sprinkle with lemon juice and season with salt and pepper.
Mix the mustard and mayonnaise and spoon over salad. Toss lightly.

Chopped-ham-and-cheeseburger

¼ cup cooked ham, diced

2 tbsp. grated Cheddar cheese

1 tbsp. finely chopped shallot

1 hard-cooked egg, finely chopped

2 stuffed olives, chopped

1 tbsp. mayonnaise

1 tbsp. chili sauce

1 hamburger bun, buttered

Preheat oven to 450°F.

Combine all the ingredients and place mixture between two halves of hamburger bun.

Wrap in aluminum foil and bake 10 – 15 minutes.

Crab salad in scallop shell

1 – 2 lettuce leaves

1 can crabmeat (5 oz.)

½ cup canned mixed vegetables

1 tbsp. mayonnaise

Pinch of paprika

Line a scallop shell with lettuce leaves.

Place the drained crabmeat in the centre and surround with vegetables mixed with mayonnaise.

Garnish with a dollop of mayonnaise and sprinkle lightly with paprika.

Ham boats with asparagus and cheese

1 small French stick or submarine roll

1 tbsp. butter or margarine

2 tbsp. grated Gruyère cheese

1 tbsp. whipping cream

1 slice cooked ham, cut in two

4 canned asparagus tips, drained

Salt and pepper

Preheat oven to 400°F.

Cut the roll in two, lengthwise, scoop out the centre, and lightly butter the inside of each half.

Bake 5 minutes.

Blend the grated cheese with the whipping cream.

Place a ham slice and two asparagus tips in each half and spread the cheese mixture over.

Season with salt and pepper.

Bake 5 minutes.

Ham on rye

⅓ cup finely grated cabbage

1 tbsp. mayonnaise

½ tsp. prepared mustard

2 stuffed olives, chopped

2 slices cooked ham

2 slices rye bread

Mix the cabbage, mayonnaise, mustard, and olives.

Place the ham on a buttered slice of rye bread.

Spread cabbage mixture over, and top with second slice buttered rye bread.

Italian salad

1 cup finely chopped iceberg lettuce

1 cup finely chopped romaine lettuce

2 tbsp. chopped celery

2 tbsp. chopped green pepper

1 tbsp. sliced radish

1 tomato, quartered

1 shallot, chopped

1 tbsp. salad oil

1 tsp. tarragon vinegar

1 tsp. chopped parsley

Salt and pepper to taste

2 – 3 anchovy fillets

Combine the vegetables in a salad bowl.

Blend the oil, vinegar, parsley, salt, and pepper and pour over salad. Toss lightly.

Garnish with anchovy fillets

Lobster salad in scallop shell

1 can lobster meat (5 oz.)

2 tbsp. whisky

1 hard-cooked egg, finely chopped

2 tbsp. mayonnaise

2 tbsp. ketchup

1 – 2 lettuce leaves

Chopped parsley

Sprinkle well-drained lobster meat with whisky.

Add the chopped egg, mayonnaise, and ketchup and mix well.

Line a scallop shell with 1 – 2 lettuce leaves and mound the lobster mixture in the centre.

Sprinkle with chopped parsley.

Variation: canned crabmeat

Salmon salad

⅓ cup cucumber strips

Salt

1 small tin salmon, drained

1 lettuce leaf

¼ cup mayonnaise

Pinch of cayenne pepper

1 hard-cooked egg, quartered

2 stuffed olives, sliced

½ tsp. chopped chervil

Lightly salt the cucumber to drain excess moisture.

Combine the salmon and cucumber and place on lettuce leaf in small salad bowl.

Blend the mayonnaise and cayenne pepper and spoon over.

Garnish with egg wedges and olive slices.

Sprinkle with chopped chervil.

Serve very cold.

Seafood salad

1 can crabmeat (5 oz.), drained

½ cup large shrimp, cooked

¼ cup finely chopped lettuce

2 tbsp. French salad dressing

1 hard-cooked egg, quartered

2 stuffed olives, sliced

Combine the crab, shrimp, and chopped lettuce.
Pour the salad dressing over and toss lightly.
Garnish with egg wedges and olive slices.

Shrimp and apple salad

1 medium apple, peeled and cored

2 tbsp. lemon juice

1 can shrimp (4 oz.)

1 cup finely chopped lettuce

¼ cup whipping cream

1 tsp. prepared mustard

Salt and pepper to taste

1 tsp. chopped chervil

Dice the apple and sprinkle with 1 tablespoon lemon juice.

Rinse the shrimp in cold water and drain well.

Place the chopped lettuce, diced apple, and shrimp in a small salad bowl.

Blend the whipping cream, mustard, salt, pepper, and remaining tablespoon of lemon juice and pour over. Toss lightly.

Shrimp salad supreme

1 small potato
2 tbsp. apple juice
1 small apple, peeled and diced
1 small endive, finely chopped
1 slice cooked ham, cut in strips
1 shallot, chopped
1 can shrimp (4 oz.)
¼ cup cream
1 tbsp. lemon juice
1 tsp. prepared mustard
Salt and pepper to taste
Chopped parsley
1 hard-cooked egg, quartered

Scrub the potato and cook in salted, boiling water.

Peel, dice, and sprinkle with apple juice. Chill.

Combine the apple, endive, ham strips, shallot, drained shrimp, and chilled potato in a salad bowl.

Blend the cream, lemon juice, mustard, salt, and pepper and pour over salad. Toss lightly.

Sprinkle with chopped parsley and garnish with egg wedges.

Submarine sandwich

1 small French stick or submarine roll

1 lettuce leaf

1 oz. Cheddar cheese, cut in thin strips

1 slice cooked ham

1 slice salami

1 hard-cooked egg, sliced

1 tbsp. French salad dressing

Cut the roll lengthwise, without cutting through the bottom crust.

Butter the inside of each half.

On the bottom half, place a lettuce leaf, the cheese strips, and the slices of ham, salami, and egg. Sprinkle with French salad dressing.

Cover with the top half of the French stick.

Swiss salad

⅓ cup diced Gruyère cheese

1 cup finely chopped lettuce

½ cup cooked potato, diced

2 slices cooked ham, diced

3 tbsp. sour cream

½ tsp. prepared mustard

½ tsp. lemon juice

Salt and pepper to taste

1 hard-cooked egg, quartered

1 tsp. chopped chives

Combine the first four ingredients and mix well.

Blend the sour cream, mustard, lemon juice, salt, and pepper. Pour over the salad and toss lightly.

Garnish with egg wedges and sprinkle with chopped chives.

Tomato stuffed with crabmeat

1 large tomato

Salt

1 can crabmeat (5 oz.), drained

2 tbsp. mayonnaise

Pinch of cayenne pepper

1 tbsp. whisky

Slice the top off the tomato, scoop out the pulp, sprinkle the inside with salt, and invert to drain (10 minutes).
Stuff the tomato with a mixture of crabmeat, mayonnaise, cayenne pepper, and whiskey.
Serve well chilled.

Tuna fish and rice salad

1 tin tuna fish (7 oz.), drained

⅓ cup cooked rice

¼ cup sliced sweet pickles

1 tbsp. pickle juice

2 tbsp. salad oil

1 tsp. prepared mustard

1 tsp. tarragon

Salt and pepper to taste

1 – 2 lettuce leaves

1 tomato, quartered

Combine tuna fish, rice, and pickles.

Blend pickle juice, oil, mustard, tarragon, salt, and pepper and pour dressing over tuna fish mixture.

Place salad on a bed of lettuce leaves and garnish with tomato wedges.

Tuna fish salad

1 tbsp. vinegar

2 tbsp. salad oil

1 tsp. prepared mustard

Salt and pepper to taste

1 medium potato

1 can tuna fish (7 oz.), drained

1 shallot, chopped

1 tsp. chopped parsley

1 hard-cooked egg, quartered

4 stuffed olives, sliced

Blend the vinegar, oil, mustard, salt, and pepper. Refrigerate.
Scrub the potato well and cook in salted, boiling water.
Peel, dice, and sprinkle with refrigerated dressing.
Add the tuna fish, shallot, and parsley and toss lightly.
Garnish with egg wedges and olive slices.

Waldorf salad

½ cup diced apple

¼ cup chopped celery

⅓ cup green grapes, halved

2 tbsp. chopped nuts

1 cup finely chopped lettuce

1 tbsp. mayonnaise

Combine all the ingredients in a small salad bowl and mix well.
Serve well chilled.

Desserts

Apple tarts

4 frozen tart shells

1 apple, peeled and cored

Lemon juice

4 tsp. brown sugar

8 tsp. red currant jelly

Preheat oven to 375°F.

Bake the shells according to the directions on the package.

Cut the apple in thin slices. Sprinkle with lemon juice to prevent browning.

Divide the apple slices evenly among the baked tart shells. Sprinkle each with 1 teaspoon brown sugar and bake for 10 – 15 minutes.

Remove from oven and spoon 2 tablespoons red currant jelly over each, letting the jelly melt in.

Bananas in Cointreau

2 tbsp. red currant jelly

1 tbsp. Cointreau

1 banana, sliced

Mix the red currant jelly and Cointreau and pour over banana slices.
Refrigerate for one hour before serving.

Bananas and cream cheese

1 medium banana, sliced

1 tbsp. lemon juice

3 oz. cream cheese

3 tbsp. whipping cream

2 tbsp. sugar

½ tsp. vanilla

Sprinkle sliced banana with lemon juice.
Blend the cream cheese, whipping cream, sugar, and vanilla and mix gently
with banana slices.

Blueberry parfait

½ cup vanilla pudding

2 tbsp. sour cream

⅔ cup blueberry pie filling

Make the pudding according to directions on the package. Fold in the sour cream.

Fill two parfait glasses with alternating layers of pudding and blueberry pie filling. Refrigerate 10 – 15 minutes.

Keep the second parfait in the refrigerator for dessert the next day or for a light snack.

The unused pie filling will keep very well in a tightly sealed container in the refrigerator. You can use it as a spread for toast or pancakes or as a topping for ice cream.

To use the rest of the vanilla pudding, see the recipe for:

Peach cream, page 198

Cherry tarts

4 frozen tart shells

Cherry pie filling, canned

Whipped cream, sweetened

Bake the tart shells according to the directions on the package.

Fill the shells with cherry pie filling and garnish with sweetened whipped cream.

Variations: blueberry, strawberry, raspberry, peach, or any other pie filling may be used.

The rest of the canned cherry pie filling can be used as a topping for ice cream or as a spread for toast or pancakes.

Coconut fruit cup

1 small banana, sliced

2 slices canned pineapple, drained and cubed

2 tbsp. orange juice

1 tbsp. coconut, toasted

Mix the bananas and pineapple and sprinkle with orange juice.
Serve well chilled in a small dessert dish, garnished with toasted coconut.

Fried banana

1 medium banana

1 tbsp. butter or margarine

1 tbsp. sugar

2 tbsp. orange juice

2 tbsp. sweetened condensed milk

Cut the banana in half lengthwise and fry in hot butter until golden brown.

Sprinkle sugar over and cook until it has caramelized.

Place the banana halves on a heated plate.

Deglaze the pan with orange juice and condensed milk and pour the sauce over the bananas. Serve immediately.

Fruit custard

1 egg

1 tbsp. sugar

1 tbsp. flour

½ cup scalded milk

2 tsp. light rum

¼ cup fruit cocktail, well drained

1 maraschino cherry

Beat the egg with sugar and flour. Add the scalded milk, slowly, and cook over low heat until the mixture thickens. Stir in the rum, cover with wax paper, and refrigerate.

When the custard is thoroughly chilled, add fruit cocktail.

Serve in a parfait glass, garnished with a maraschino cherry.

Use the rest of the canned fruit cocktail in:

Fruit salad, page 195

Fruit salad

1 tbsp. sour cream

¼ tsp. almond extract

1 tsp. sugar

¾ cup canned fruit cocktail, drained

1 tbsp. shredded coconut, toasted

Put the fruit cocktail into a dessert bowl.

Combine the sour cream, almond extract, and sugar and mix into the fruit.

Sprinkle with toasted coconut.

Green grapes in sour cream

1 cup seedless green grapes

2 tbsp. sour cream

1 tbsp. brown sugar

Mix the grapes and sour cream and place the mixture in a dessert dish.
Sprinkle with brown sugar and refrigerate.

Orange slices in apple juice

1 orange, peeled

1 tsp. sugar

1 tbsp. lemon juice

3 tbsp. apple juice

Cut the orange in thin slices, crosswise, and put in a dessert dish. Sprinkle with sugar and toss in lemon and apple juice.

Refrigerate until ready to serve.

Peach cream

1 peach, peeled

⅓ cup vanilla pudding

1 tbsp. sour cream

1 maraschino cherry

Cut the peach in two and remove the pit. Cut each peach half in slices and place in a dessert dish.
Fold the sour cream into the pudding and spoon over peach slices.
Garnish with a maraschino cherry.

Peach macaroon

1 fresh peach, peeled, or 2 halves, canned and well drained

1 coconut macaroon

1 tbsp. red currant jelly

1 tbsp. chopped nuts

3 oz. cream cheese

3 tbsp. whipping cream

2 tbsp. sugar

½ tsp. vanilla

Cut the peach in two and remove the pit.

Crumble the macaroon and mix with the jelly and nuts.

Fill each peach half with this mixture, put the two halves together, and place in a dessert bowl.

With a wire whip or fork, beat the cream cheese, whipping cream, sugar, and vanilla until smooth. Spoon over peach.

Serve well chilled.

Peach Melba

1 fresh peach, peeled

Vanilla ice cream

2 – 3 tbsp. raspberry jam

Cut the peach in two and remove the pit.

Top each peach half with vanilla ice cream and raspberry jam.

Variations: canned peach halves, well drained, or fresh or canned pears

Peach à la mode

2 peach halves, canned or fresh

Vanilla ice cream

1 tbsp. strawberry jam

Top each peach half with ice cream and jam. (If using a fresh peach, peel first.)

Pears and apple sauce

2 pear halves, canned and drained

2 tbsp. apple sauce

1 tbsp. white rum

1 tbsp. toasted almonds

Place the pear halves in a dessert bowl.
Combine the apple sauce and rum and pour over.
Garnish with toasted almonds.
Serve well chilled.

Pears in apricot syrup

2 pears halves, canned and drained

1 tbsp. pear syrup

1 tbsp. apricot jam or marmalade

1 tbsp. sugar

Place the pear halves in a dessert dish.

Heat the syrup, marmalade, and sugar in a small saucepan for 2 – 3 minutes.

Pour over the pears and refrigerate until ready to serve.

Pears in cognac

2 pear halves, canned and drained

2 tbsp. pear syrup

1 tsp. sugar

1 tbsp. cognac

Pinch of pepper

Place the pear halves in a dessert bowl.

Bring the syrup and sugar to a rapid boil and let boil for 2 – 3 seconds.

Add the cognac and pepper and pour over the pears.

Refrigerate until well chilled.

Pears in sour cream syrup

2 pear halves, canned and drained

2 tbsp. pear syrup

1 tsp. butter or margarine

1 tbsp. sour cream

Place the pear halves in a dessert bowl.

Bring the syrup to a rapid boil. Add the butter and sour cream and heat for a few minutes, stirring.

Pour over the pears and refrigerate until well chilled.

Pears in syrup

2 pear halves, canned

2 tsp. strawberry jam

2 tbsp. pear syrup

1 tbsp. sugar

Drain the pear halves thoroughly and fill the cavity of each with strawberry jam.

Put the syrup and sugar in a small saucepan and bring to a rapid boil. Pour over the pears and refrigerate until ready to serve.

Pineapple and cream cheese

3 oz. cream cheese

1 tbsp. whipping cream

2 tbsp. sugar

2 slices pineapple

1 maraschino cherry

Blend the cream and sugar into the cheese with a fork.

Spoon onto the pineapple slices and garnish with the maraschino cherry.

Pineapple and honey

2 tbsp. sour cream

2 tbsp. honey

3 slices pineapple, cubed

1 maraschino cherry, cut in two

Mix the sour cream and honey and spoon over pineapple cubes. Garnish with maraschino cherry.

Serve very cold.

Pineapple and ice cream

2 slices canned pineapple, drained

1 thick slice vanilla ice cream

1 tbsp. apricot jam

1 tbsp. toasted almonds

Place the slice of ice cream between the pineapple slices. Spread apricot jam over and garnish with toasted almonds.

The rest of the canned pineapple can be used in the dessert recipes that follow or in these recipes:
Hawaiian hamburger, page 57
Broiled ham with pineapple, page 71

Pineapple and orange in Cointreau

1 orange, peeled and diced

2 tbsp. Cointreau

2 tsp. sugar

1 tbsp. lemon juice

1 slice pineapple

Marinate the diced orange in a mixture of the Cointreau, sugar, and lemon juice in the refrigerator for about an hour.

Place a slice of chilled pineapple in a small dessert dish and pour the orange and marinade over.

Raspberry parfait

½ cup milk

½ cup sour cream

¼ cup lemon instant pudding powder

Fresh raspberries

Blend the milk and sour cream.

Add the pudding powder and beat until smooth.

Fill two parfait glasses with alternating layers of pudding and raspberries.

Keep the second parfait in the refrigerator for dessert the next day or for a light snack.

The unused portion of the pudding mix should be tightly resealed so that it does not cake or harden.

Raspberry yoghurt parfait

¼ cup whipping cream

1 serving raspberry yoghurt

Whip the cream and fold into the yoghurt, reserving 1 tablespoon of the
whipped cream for garnish.
Serve in a parfait glass.

Strawberry delight

½ cup strawberry yoghurt

1 tbsp. sugar

2 – 3 drops red food coloring

⅔ cup sliced strawberries

Mix the yoghurt, sugar, and food coloring and pour over strawberries.
Serve well chilled.

Yoghurt fruit cup

¼ cup orange, diced

⅓ cup banana, sliced

1 tbsp. sugar

2 tbsp. whipping cream

1 tbsp. yoghurt

1 tbsp. raspberry jelly

Mix the orange and banana and sprinkle with sugar.

Lightly whip the cream. Fold in the yoghurt and fruit mixture.

Put into a dessert bowl, garnish with raspberry jelly, and refrigerate until ready to serve.

Miscellaneous

Cheesy rice

2 tbsp. chopped onion

2 slices bacon, diced

1 tsp. oil

1 cup cooked rice

2 tbsp. grated Gruyère cheese

Salt and pepper to taste

Sauté the onion and bacon in hot oil. Add the rice, cheese, salt, and pepper and stir-fry until well mixed and heated through.

This rice goes well with fish dishes.

Croissants with egg-cheese spread

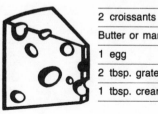

2 croissants
Butter or margarine
1 egg
2 tbsp. grated Gruyère cheese
1 tbsp. cream

Preheat oven to 375°F.

Cut the croissants in two and butter each half.

Beat the egg, cheese, and cream. Spread over two bottom halves and cover with two top halves.

Bake in a small buttered baking dish for 10 minutes.

This makes a tasty snack as well as a nourishing breakfast.

Mushroom sauce

1 tbsp. butter or margarine

1 tbsp. finely chopped onion

1 tbsp. mushrooms, sliced

¼ cup beef consommé

1 tbsp. ketchup

2 tsp. HP sauce

½ tsp. tarragon

Salt and pepper to taste

1 tsp. cornstarch

Brown the onion and mushrooms in hot butter. Add the next five ingredients and bring rapidly to a boil.

Thicken the sauce by stirring in the cornstarch dissolved in a little cold water.

Mustard sauce

¼ cup sour cream

1 tbsp. onion soup mix

1 tsp. prepared mustard

Combine the ingredients in a small saucepan and cook over low heat, stirring, until the sauce begins to boil.
Serve with ham.

Oil and vinegar dressing

¼ cup oil

2 tbsp. wine vinegar

Salt and pepper

1 small garlic clove, crushed

Put all the ingredients in a jar with a tight-fitting lid. Shake well. Keep refrigerated.

Parslied rice

½ cup quick-cooking rice

½ cup boiling water

Salt and pepper to taste

1 tbsp. butter or margarine

1 tbsp. chopped parsley

Prepare the rice according to the directions on the package, but using ½ cup of boiling water.

Add the remaining ingredients and mix well.

Provençal sauce

1 small tomato, quartered
¼ tsp. sugar
1 shallot, chopped
2 tbsp. butter or margarine
1 tbsp. sherry
Pinch of ground cloves
1 tsp. chopped parsley
Salt and pepper

Sprinkle the tomato with sugar and set aside.

Sauté the shallot in 1 tablespoon butter. Add the sherry and tomato and heat for a minute or two.

Add the remaining tablespoon of butter, cloves, and parsley. Stir until the butter is completely melted. Season with salt and pepper.

Serve with steak.

Quick barbecue sauce

¼ cup ketchup

1 tbsp. butter or margarine

1 tbsp. molasses

2 tsp. vinegar

1 tbsp. water

Combine all the ingredients in a small saucepan and bring to a boil. Simmer
for 3 – 4 minutes.

Quick tartar sauce

2 tbsp. mayonnaise

1 tbsp. sweet relish

Blend the mayonnaise and relish.
Serve with fried fish.

Rice with almonds

¼ cup long-grain rice

1 tbsp. slivered almonds

2 tbsp. finely chopped onion

1 tbsp. butter or margarine

½ cup chicken bouillon

Sauté the rice, almonds, and onion in hot butter for 5 minutes, stirring.
Pour in the chicken bouillon, cover, and cook over low heat 20 – 30 minutes,
until the liquid is absorbed and the rice tender.

Rice with mushrooms

½ cup quick-cooking rice

2 tbsp. butter or margarine

¼ cup sliced mushrooms

2 tsp. chopped parsley

Salt and pepper to taste

Cook the rice according to the directions on the package.

Sauté the mushrooms in 1 tablespoon butter. Keep hot.

When the rice is cooked, add the remaining tablespoon of butter, mushrooms, parsley, salt, and pepper and mix well.

Wine sauce

1 tbsp. chopped shallot

¼ cup white wine

2 tbsp. butter or margarine

1 tsp. chopped parsley

Salt and pepper to taste

Put the shallot and wine in a small saucepan and bring rapidly to a boil. Cook about one minute.

Remove from heat, add the remaining ingredients, and stir until the butter is completely melted.

Serve with steak.